Gifts of Nature

✦ TREES *of* ✦
CHRISTMAS

National Wildlife Federation

TREES OF CHRISTMAS

Library of Congress CIP Data: page 47.

The Ancients

One need not go into history to find the reasons for veneration of the evergreen tree as a part of the Christmas season. They are of the enduring things of this earth, and man has known them as long as man has been here. The pine, the spruce, the hemlock, the fir — all those conifers that know no leafless season — have been held in special favor when man would have symbols of life that outlast all winters.

We gather them now, even as the ancients gathered them reaching for the reassurance of enduring green life at the time of the winter solstice. We are reaching for reassurance, for the beauty of the living green but also for that green itself, the green of life that outlasts the gray winds, the white frosts, and the glittering snow of winter.

Hal Borland

Wild Things

After a heavy snow, my evergreens stand each according to its character and habit, but all silently and with stoic calm, awaiting a change of wind or return of the sun. By their form and posture you may know them.

The junipers, of course, were overwhelmed by storm. Except for a feathery branch emerging here and there, their line might be a long drift. The thick tough branches bow down sullenly beneath the snow. And underneath the branches, there are many-footed revels as the mice disport, safe beneath branch and drift from prowling cat or plunging fox.

But the serried ranks of spruce stand like so many tepees, the sharp four-angled needles on the bristled twigs drooping only imperceptibly under the weight of snow, each branch holding what it may, then letting the surplus slide on down, creating at the heart of each tree a dim shelter for junco, finch, and chickadee.

The cedars would do likewise; they have the heart but not the stomach for it. Their tall spires maintain a stern upright stance until the scaled aromatic leaves have more than they can bear. Then suddenly the whole tower bends under the weight, sometimes almost to the ground, yet only rarely does one break. A hungry deer may thus find an exceptional lunch brought within reach, but brushing against it may dislodge the snow and let the tree snap straight again.

The big trees are different, and different from one another. Shouldering against the storm, the white pines disdain the snow. Their great clusters of long needles, five together and nearly five inches long, wave away accumulation.

On the other hand, the Norways grieve at violence. The great branches with their plumes of dark doubled needles sigh at the coming of the wind; and when they are heavy with snow, the branches bend this way and that, unpredictably, creating a haven for huddling beast or even man, away from the cutting edge.

Each of these conifers behaves according to a distinct pattern. Trees, like men, respond to adversity with individuality, and yet predictably, each according to its nature and how life has shaped it.

Dion Henderson

Favorite Christmas Trees

There is no "best" Christmas tree. It all depends on your taste in shape, needles, and scent. Americans bought more than 34 million natural Christmas trees in 1987, according to the National Christmas Tree Assn. Ninety percent were grown in the U.S., with Oregon producing the most, followed by Michigan, Wisconsin, California, and North Carolina.

Many tree-farms are family-owned and run. Most growers buy one- or two-year-old trees from nurseries, plant them in close rows and later transplant them. During their growing period—from five to ten years—the trees are sheared to give a full and bushy look with a tapered top.

When choosing a Christmas tree, look for green needles that bend easily but don't break or fall off. Give the trunk a fresh, straight cut and place the tree in a water-holding stand. If the base of the trunk dries out, a seal will form and the tree will not hold its color or moisture.

After Christmas, the tree need not be thrown away. Chop it and use as mulch, add it to the compost heap, or set it in the yard as a bird sanctuary.

Douglas fir

Popular in the northwest, the Douglas fir has bright green needles 1″ long. It grows rapidly in mild, humid climates. In the northeast, the *balsam fir*, with featherlike, soft needles, is extremely popular. Both varieties have cones that stand straight up on the branches.

Scotch pine

This bushy tree has stiff needles up to 3″ long, which are attached to the stem in bundles of two or three. Its cones hang down from its branches. The Scotch pine grows in the north-eastern United States and in Canada.

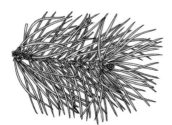

Red cedar

The red cedar has small, flat, over-lapping leaves which look like scales. Its small, hard berries are white to blackish-green in color. The cedar thrives in limestone regions, but also will grow well in poor, dry soil.

Norway spruce

Most spruce have prickly needles that grow all around the twig. This variety, often sold as a live Christmas tree, grows into a tree with long, sweeping branches when transplanted.

The Enduring Evergreens

Grandparents and newlyweds, toddlers and teenagers—all delight in the custom of decorating the Christmas tree. Yet evergreens are even more important in their natural setting. In the northern pine forests, martens dash through the branches, hunting squirrels and birds. Mourning doves, hawks, and cardinals all build their nests in evergreens; squirrels and white-footed mice do the same. Great horned owls show a decided preference for large white pines or hemlocks for nesting. When winter storms blow, deer, ruffed grouse, and bobwhites find shelter under evergreens' dense branches.

Evergreens supply food as well as shelter. Snowshoe hares munch on spruce needles, while in the Northwest, Douglas squirrels gnaw the stem of a green pinecone until the cone drops. Then the squirrels scamper down the tree to dig out the fallen cone's seeds or to cache it for a hungrier day. Pine grosbeaks use their stout, sharp-edged bills to cut into the cone, while the piñon jay finds most of his fare on the ground beneath the trees.

Conifers aren't indestructible, of course. Porcupines gnaw great patches of bark from pine to uncover the tasty inner bark. Several years ago, a porcupine population explosion in Vermont began to endanger the pine forests. The state finally imported the porcupine's only natural enemy, the fisher, a flesh-eating animal of the marten family. Today the porcupines are back in balance and the pine and fir forests are no longer in danger.

And the evergreens have survived because of defenses against the damage insects can cause. In balsam firs, a compound mimics the hormone that controls growth in insects. When a caterpillar munches on the ersatz hormone, it is doomed to a life of immaturity, never becoming an adult and never reproducing. Some evergreens use another defense: sticky resin that traps munching insects. Over millions of years, blobs of pine resin have hardened into tawny amber gems, inside of which an ancient insect is often perfectly preserved.

Home to thousands of animals, evergreens are among nature's oldest, sturdiest creations. When the Egyptians were building the pyramids more than 4,000 years ago, the bristlecone pines in California's White Mountains were already seedlings.

Evergreens tenaciously hang on, even in harsh climates, while other trees turn brown. That has made them a symbol of strength in many cultures. One legend tells of a North Dakota Indian tribe which each spring planted a cedar near the medicine lodge. Children hung gifts on the little tree, such as a finely woven shawl or moccasins. When fall arrived, the tree was dug up and, with great ceremony, set afloat on a long journey down the Missouri.

Though they are well suited to winter, the trees are as at home in the Arizona desert as they are beside a mountain lake. Conifers survive winter's wind and ice because of hard, tough-skinned needles that continue food production all year. Their skinny needles and waxy coating keep too much snow from sticking. When snow does pile up, the branches dip, shrugging it off.

During arid summers, evergreens on mountaintops survive well because of their ability to absorb moisture from clouds. Balsam firs and spruce have a large surface area where moisture can condense and be held. Summer fog as well condenses on the needles, drips down, and waters the tree.

The conifers also have survived because they reproduce themselves in a system that takes advantage of the wind and the design of the cone. If the pollen fails to land on one scale of a pine cone, it is passed on to the next scale, increasing the chances that a young seedling will result. Thus the resilient evergreen reproduces itself, a sturdy symbol not only of Christmas, but of enduring life.

Richard Wolkomir

The Christmas Tree Tradition

Each December rows of Christmas trees, their branches unfolding after a journey tightly-wrapped, stand on street corners across America. Gloved hands stomp the trunks on the hard earth, careful buyers bend the needles to test their freshness. In America last year alone, 34 million trees—durable Douglas firs, fragrant balsams, Norway spruce, and popular Scotch pines—were carted home and decorated.

Yet this popular custom has not always been a part of the American Christmas. Instead, the story of evergreens and Christmas is a series of small beginnings and delightful legends.

Special powers. That's what some Old World Europeans thought the evergreens contained, because the trees stayed green while the rest of the forest turned brown. During winter solstice, people decorated their homes with evergreen boughs and danced around bonfires to entice the sun to warm the earth again.

As Christianity spread, church leaders first frowned on the pagan custom. But later they just adapted this popular tradition, and the tree evolved into a symbol of the Christian holiday.

The custom was especially popular with the Germans, who decorated trees with stars and bells, candles and cookies. It became even more popular, especially with Lutherans, thanks to a legend that identified the tree with theologian Martin Luther. According to an apocryphal story, the crusty rebel was out walking on Christmas Eve when he chopped down a fir tree and lugged it home, then put numerous candles on it to impress his son with the message that the Christ Child was the light of the world.

In 1845, almost 300 years after Luther's death, an artist painted Luther's family around a shining, candle-covered Christmas tree. As the painting became popular, so did the custom of the decorated Christmas tree—at least in Germany.

The English had never particularly taken to the notion, perhaps because not many evergreens were readily available. But one engraving in the 1848 *Illustrated London News* changed all that. It showed Queen Victoria and her husband, Prince Albert, beside a richly decorated evergreen. The

Spun-glass butterfly ornament.

tree was Albert's idea. Born in Germany, he was perhaps nostalgic about Christmases in the past. When English readers saw the magazine, they adopted the Christmas tree tradition as their own. Although Germany deserves credit for popularizing the Christmas tree, the custom was slow to take hold among settlers who came to the New World.

The Puritans who settled in Massachusetts certainly didn't abide such holiday levity. In 1659 they banned any celebrations with this stern decree: "Whosoever shall be found observing any such day as Christmas . . . shall pay five shillings." In 1681, the law was repealed, but December 25 remained a working day.

The first true Christmas trees we know of in America were in the German Moravian community at Bethlehem, Pennsylvania, in 1747. A hand-scrawled diary tells us that "for this occasion several pyramids of green brushwood had been prepared, all decorated with candles and the large one with apples and pretty verses."

Another account, printed in an 1832 Sunday-school pamphlet, also helped alert Americans to the new holiday custom. "The tree was the top of a

young fir," wrote one Boston observer. "Smart dolls and other whimsies glittered and there was not a twig which had not something sparkling upon it. The effect of opening the doors . . . was delightful. The children poured in, but in a moment every voice was hushed. At last, a quick pair of eyes discovered that it bore something eatable, and from that moment the babble began. . . ."

Most trees in early America were decorated with cookies, candy, pine cones, and strings of popcorn and cranberries. When a settler named Gustave Koerner found himself on an Illinois riverbank devoid of fir trees in the mid-1800s, he improvised. He decorated a sassafras tree with ribbons, hazelnuts, and polished red haws, the fruit of the hawthorn tree.

The American tree was transformed, however, by German-made glass balls and icicles, which probably reached America around 1860, transported along with the treasured possessions of immigrant families. By the turn of the century, dozens of designs tempted American shoppers.

Some of the most charming ones were the silver

and gold embossed cardboard "Dresden ornaments." Customers could choose from an exotic collection of fish, polar bears, camels, eagles, suns, elephants, and even alligators. These marvels usually stood only two to three inches high, but one could still make out the details of a donkey's hair or an elephant's wrinkles.

German glassblowers reproduced apples, pinecones, monkeys, and bears—and eager American buyers snapped them up. These fragile, hand-blown ornaments also took the shape of cockatoos, parrots, butterflies, peacocks, and owls.

Painted papier-mache fishes, up to 15 inches long, appeared on trees in New England. Open a trap door, and out flowed candy to delight a child.

Until the middle of the nineteenth century any family who had a Christmas tree either cut it themselves or ordered it from a farmer. But in 1851, a man named Mark Carr changed all that. All around him in New York's Catskill Mountains, Carr saw trees free for the taking. Carr and his sons loaded two oxsleds with firs and spruces and put them on a steamboat bound for New York. A silver dollar secured the rent of a small strip of sidewalk in New York's Washington Market. Before long, customers were flocking to purchase the novelties—at city-slicker prices.

Carr had launched the nation's first Christmas

tree lot. By 1880, more than 600 tree dealers competed for space along the dockfront. The trees were piled up like cord wood, or they stood on butt ends in long rows for several blocks. Sidewalks were walled in behind hills of trees that excluded the sunlight, compelling storekeepers to use gaslights even at midday.

Different years saw different styles. Cedar trees were popular until the 1880s, when the fashion switched to evergreens that created less of a fire hazard when lighted with candles.

By 1900, only one American family in five had a Christmas tree, although most children probably enjoyed one at school, church, or a neighbor's house. By 1930, however, the tree had become a commonplace part of the American Christmas, not just in private homes but

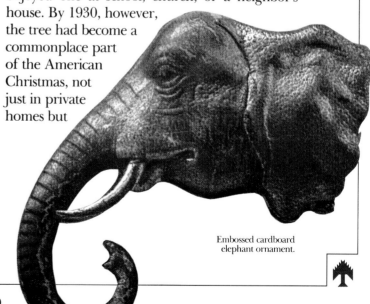

Embossed cardboard
elephant ornament.

in community parks, businesses, and even in the dignified halls of the White House.

Not all presidents were quick to join in the enthusiasm, however. An ardent conservationist, Theodore Roosevelt worried about the random cutting of evergreens. He was chagrined one Christmas to find that his young son, Archie, had smuggled a tree into the White House.

Roosevelt wrote a friend: "Yesterday morning the children began to hammer at the door of their mother's and my room, in which their stockings, all bulging out with queer angles, were hanging from the fireplace. But first there was a surprise . . . for Archie had a little Christmas tree, which he had rigged up with the help of one of the carpenters in a closet."

Roosevelt sent Archie and his brother, Quentin, to conservationist Gifford Pinchot, hoping that Pinchot would give the boys a lecture. Instead, Pinchot told them that the cutting of Christmas trees could help in thinning timberlands. This was the first of many times Pinchot and the Forest Service would defend the Christmas tree against its critics. Sound conservation practices became more prevalent, and for many farmers, Christmas tree cultivation became a profitable business.

For years, the best-selling tree had been the Douglas fir. But in the Depression years, a new type of Christmas tree made its debut. An entrepreneur named Fred Musser planted Scotch pines on abandoned Pennsylvania farms, hoping to sell them for Christmas. Musser knew long-needled pines would be more difficult to decorate than trees with short needles. On the other hand, cut Scotch pines will keep their needles for days, whereas balsams and spruces start dropping their needles practically the moment they feel the axe.

In 1930 Musser loaded 11 railroad cars with his Scotch pines and shipped them to a dealer in New York. He calculated that the trees were worth $11,000, yet he got only $198 for the lot of them. Undismayed, he told his partners: "We've got a lot more missionary work to do with this product." Under his prodding, markets opened up; by the 1970s, Fred Musser's long-needled Scotch pine became America's most popular Christmas tree.

Ancient custom, modern twists. In the late 1980s, a grower in Maine sold about 1,500 mail order trees, mostly balsam firs, at $40 each. City dwellers without cars snapped them up, as did a few families shipping to servicemen overseas.

Then there's Ikea, a home-furnishings store on the east coast which rented out Canadian balsams for $10 plus a $10 deposit. Upon return, the store refunded the $10—then ground up the returned trees for garden mulch.   *Phillip Snyder*

For Allan

Who wanted to see how I wrote a poem.

Among these mountains, do you know,
I have a farm, and on it grow
A thousand lovely Christmas trees.
I'd like to send you one of these,
But it's against the laws.
A man may give a little boy
A book, a useful knife, a toy,
Or even a rhyme like this by me
(I write it just like this you see).
But nobody may give a tree
Excepting Santa Claus.

Robert Frost

*A young boy, Allan Neilson, had indicated
a desire to know how Robert Frost wrote
his poems. Around 1917, Frost penned this
reply on a card.*

22

little tree

little tree
little silent Christmas tree
you are so little
you are more like a flower

who found you in the green forest
and were you very sorry to come away?
see   i will comfort you
because you smell so sweetly

i will kiss your cool bark
and hug you safe and tight
just as your mother would,
only don't be afraid

look   the spangles
that sleep all the year in a dark box
dreaming of being taken out and allowed to shine,
the balls the chains red and gold the fluffy threads,

put up your little arms
and i'll give them all to you to hold
every finger shall have its ring
and there won't be a single place dark or unhappy

then when you're quite dressed
you'll stand in the window for everyone to see
and how they'll stare!
oh but you'll be very proud

and my little sister and i will take hands
and looking up at our beautiful tree
we'll dance and sing
"Noel Noel"

e.e. cummings

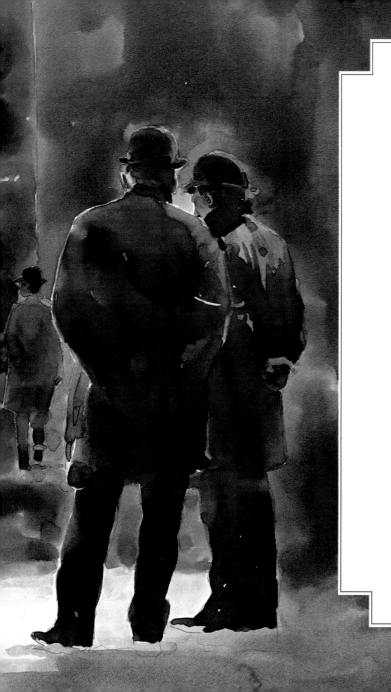

Francie's Christmas

Christmas was a charmed time in Brooklyn. The spruce trees began coming into Francie Nolan's neighborhood the week before Christmas. Their branches were corded to make shipping easier. Vendors rented space on the curb before a store and stretched a rope from pole to pole and leaned the trees against it. All day they walked up and down this one-sided avenue of aromatic leaning trees, blowing on stiff ungloved fingers. And the air was cold and still, and full of the pine smell and the smell of tangerines which appeared in the stores only at Christmas time and the mean street was truly wonderful for a little while.

There was a cruel custom in the neighborhood. At midnight on the Eve of our dear Saviour's birth, the kids gathered where there were unsold trees. There was a saying that if you waited until then, you wouldn't have to buy a tree; that "they'd chuck 'em at you." This was literally true.

The man threw each tree in turn, starting with the biggest. Kids volunteered to stand up against the throwing. If a boy didn't fall down under the impact, the tree was his. If he fell, he forfeited his chance at winning a tree. Only the roughest boys and some of the young men elected to be hit by the big trees. The others waited shrewdly until a tree came up that they could stand against. The littlest kids waited for the tiny, foot-high trees and shrieked in delight when they won one.

On the Christmas Eve when Francie was ten and her brother, Neeley, nine, Mama consented to let them go down and have their first try for a tree. Francie had picked out her tree earlier in the day. She had stood near it all afternoon and evening praying that no one would buy it. To her joy, it was still there at midnight. It was the biggest tree in the neighborhood and its price was so high that no one could afford to buy it. It was ten feet high. Its branches were bound with new white rope and it came to a sure pure point at its top. The man took this tree out first.

Before Francie could speak up, a neighborhood bully, a boy of eighteen known as Punky Perkins, stepped forward and ordered the man to chuck the tree at him. The man hated the way Punky was so confident. He looked around and asked, "Anybody else wanna take a chanct on it?"

Francie stepped forward. "Me, Mister."

A spurt of derisive laughter came from the tree man. The kids snickered. A few adults who had gathered to watch the fun guffawed. "Aw g'wan. You're too little," the tree man objected.

"Me and my brother—we're not too little together," Francie said.

She pulled Neeley forward. The tree man looked at them—a thin girl of ten with starveling hollows in her cheeks but with the chin still baby-round. He looked at the little boy with his fair hair and round blue eyes—Neeley Nolan, all innocence and trust.

"Two ain't fair," yelped Punky.

"Shut your lousy trap," advised the man who held all power in that hour. "These here kids is got nerve. Stand back, the rest of youse. These kids is goin' to have a show at this tree."

The others made a wavering lane. Francie and Neeley stood at one end of it and the big man at the other. It was a human funnel with Francie and her brother making the small end of it.

The man flexed his great arms to throw the great tree. He noticed how tiny the children looked at the end of the short lane. For the split part of a moment, the tree thrower went through a kind of Gethsemane.

"Oh, why don't I just give 'em the tree, say Merry Christmas and let 'em go?" his soul agonized. "What's the tree to me? I can't sell it no more this year and it won't keep till next year." The kids watched him solemnly as he stood there in his moment of thought.

"But then," he rationalized, "if I did that, all the others would expect to get 'em handed to 'em. And next year, nobody a-tall would buy a tree off of me. I ain't a big enough man to give this tree away for nothing." He finally came to his conclusion. "Oh, what the hell! Them two kids is gotta live in this world. They *got* to get used to it. They got to learn to give and to take punishment." As he threw the tree with all his strength, his heart wailed out, "It's a rotten, lousy world!"

Francie saw the tree leave his hands. There was a split bit of being when time and space had no meaning. The whole world stood still as something dark and monstrous came through the air. There was nothing — nothing but pungent darkness and something that grew and grew as it rushed at her. She staggered as the tree hit them. Neeley went to his knees but she pulled him up fiercely before he could go down. There was a mighty swishing sound as the tree settled. Everything was dark, green and prickly. Then she felt a sharp pain at the side of her head where the trunk of the tree had hit her.

When some of the older boys pulled the tree away, they found Francie and her brother standing upright, hand in hand. Blood was coming from scratches on Neeley's face. He looked more like a baby than ever with his bewildered blue eyes and the fairness of his skin made more noticeable because of the clear red blood. But they were smiling. Had they not won the biggest tree in the neighborhood? Some of the boys hollered, "Hooray!" A few adults clapped. The tree man eulogized them by screaming, "And now get the hell out of here with your tree!"

Such phrases could mean many things according to the expression and tone used in saying them. So now Francie smiled tremulously at the kind man. She knew that he was really saying, "Goodbye — God bless you."

It wasn't easy dragging that tree home. They had to pull it inch by inch. In a way, it was good that it took them so long to get the tree home. It made their triumph more drawn out. Francie glowed when a lady said, "I never saw such a big tree!" The cop on their corner stopped them, examined the tree, and solemnly offered to buy it for ten cents — fifteen cents if they'd deliver it to his home. Francie nearly burst with pride although she knew he was joking. She said she wouldn't sell it for a dollar, even.

They had to call up to Papa to help them get the

tree up the narrow stairs. Papa's amazement at the size of the tree was flattering. He pretended to believe that it wasn't theirs. Francie had a lot of fun convincing him although she knew all the while that the whole thing was make-believe. Papa pulled in front and Francie and Neeley pushed in back and they began forcing the big tree up the three flights of stairs. Papa was so excited that he started singing, not caring that it was rather late at night. He sang "Holy Night." The narrow walls took up his clear sweet voice, held it for a breath and gave it back with doubled sweetness. Doors creaked open and families gathered on the landings, pleased and amazed at the something unexpected being added to that moment of their lives.

Francie saw the Tynmore sisters standing together in their doorway, their gray hair in crimpers, and ruffled, starched nightgowns showing under their voluminous wrappers. They added their thin, poignant voices to Papa's. Floss Gaddis, her mother and her brother, Henny, who was dying of consumption, stood in their doorway. Henny was crying and when Papa saw him, he let the song trail off; he thought maybe it made Henny too sad.

Flossie was in a Klondike-dance-hall-girl costume waiting for an escort to take her to a masquerade ball which started soon after midnight.

More to make Henny smile than anything else, Papa said, "Floss, we got no angel for the top of this Christmas tree. How about you obliging?"

Floss was all ready to make a dirty reply about the wind blowing her drawers off if she was up that high. But she changed her mind. Something about the big proud tree, the beaming children and the rare good will of the neighbors made her ashamed of her unspoken reply. All she said was, "Gee, ain't you the kidder, Johnny Nolan."

They set the tree up in the front room after spreading a sheet to protect the carpet from falling pine needles. The tree stood in a tin bucket with broken bricks to hold it upright. When the rope was cut away, the branches spread out to fill the whole room. There was no money to buy tree decorations or lights. But the great tree standing there was enough.

The room was cold. It was a poor year, that one — too poor for them to buy the extra coal for the front room stove. Every day, during the week the tree stood there, Francie put on her sweater and cap and went in and sat under the tree. She sat there and enjoyed the smell and the dark greenness of it.

Oh, the mystery of a great tree, a prisoner in a tin wash bucket in a tenement front room!

Betty Smith

Of Ox Bells and Christmas

Lunenburg County is a handsome piece of real estate on the rocky south shore of Nova Scotia, settled primarily by Germans in the 1750s. It deserves to be known for two reasons that intertwine like the spiky branches of a holly wreath. The county's combination of soil and climate has made it the center of the Christmas-tree industry in northeastern North America. In its bosky dells the steeple-shaped balsam fir—the *ne plus ultra* of Yuletide decorations—is a hardy native, springing up unrelentingly no matter how many times an area is cut over.

The other reason to celebrate Lunenburg County has to do with the fact that when the original settlers landed along the south shore, they brought with them a tradition: the castration of young bulls and the use of the resulting oxen in yoked pairs as draught animals. And a useful tradition it was, in the heavily forested, boulder-strewn places the settlers shaped into homesteads.

In the summer of 1870, John Gaetz bought the old Goudey place on Stanburne Road — 225 acres, with a house that was even then the oldest in the community. The house had, and still has, 36-inch-wide baseboards of pine that were cut on the place, and many of the doors in the house are simply single pieces of old heartwood pine.

John Gaetz was known as a good oxteamster — and there were many such in those days. The oxen he drove up to Stanburne were probably not the first to graze that hilly farm, but they are the first still well remembered.

The senior rememberer now is his grandson, Sumner Gates, the old name Gaetz having been abandoned a few generations ago as being too "Dutchy." "Since we came here the place has never been without the sight of oxen and the sound of ox bells," is the way he likes to put it, speaking quietly from his couch by the wood cookstove. "Oxteams don't just happen, you know. You've got to get the creeturs when they're small, and mate them well for size, and lead them by their halters with ropes. And then you've got to put the head yoke onto 'em. *That's* when the fun begins."

As Gates talks, surrounded by the woven smells of mincemeat pie and baking bread, he often glances out the window and seems to be listening for something. And then he hears it. The heavy, unmistakable ringing of the ox bells on the straps around the necks of Bright and Lion, at more than 2,000 pounds apiece the largest oxen in the county, as they ease up the ice-slick hill toward the farmhouse. They're led by the voice and whip of Sumner's son, Harold, the fourth Gates oxman to work the family farm. "Haugh, Lion! Haugh! Hup!" he cries as the huge beasts heave themselves forward into Sumner's view.

Forty acres of the Gates farm is set aside for a Christmas-tree lot, all of it now in balsam fir. It is maintained by cutting back the young trees and brush of other varieties so they won't crowd out or misshape the firs.

"I go into the woods in April, before the new growth starts, to do my trimming and shaping for the coming Christmas season," Harold says. "I cut the brush back with shears and an ax, and I do most of my shaping with a long knife I made out of an old crosscut saw blade. I cut downward and out from the center o'er the whole tree to make the branches even. Most are even by their nature, but I help 'em along a bit.

"Late in the fall I begin to cut and stack the trees beside my woods road. That would be the first week of November, and I'd not think it's a good day unless I cut and drag and stack 200 trees. Some men always cut with a chain saw, but I often still use an ax with a good sharp edge onto it. The sap from the cut fir smells fresh without all that gasoline and oil to get in the way, and it's so quiet without a saw that the woods are more interesting. Just the other day I was cutting, when I heard an eagle cry, and when I looked up, I saw him dive on a rabbit. And by God if he didn't miss the rabbit on the first rush but catch him by half flying and half running along the ground. If I'd been using a power saw I'd have missed the whole thing."

After Harold has piled several hundred trees, he'll go to the barn, take the yoke down, strap it to the heads of the oxen, hitch them to either a rubber-tired wooden wagon or, if there's snow on the ground, a double-runnered sled and drive them out to bring the trees up nearer the house where they can be picked up by the local wholesaler.

To a man like Harold, oxen give greater pleasure than he could ever derive from work with a machine. No doubt only someone who has raised a calf and carefully mated it, then cared for and trained it over a period of years so that it would grow from a spindly, mewling baby into half of a two-ton extension of his teamster, can understand what Harold feels. And no doubt only someone who walks every day of his life on the same paths his father, grandfather and great-grandfather walked, using in the living woods cries learned from men long dead to control the power of the yoked team, can understand what it means to find a good way to live and then, by God, hew to it.

One thing that's not hard to understand, sitting around the wood stove after a belt-stretching meal, watching the lights flickering in the emerald triangle of balsam fir in the front room and listening to a group of neighbors who've brought their guitars, spoons, harmonicas and voices to share them on a Christmas evening, is that underlying the festivities is a constant bass note of plenty. It resonates from the potato, apple and carrot bins in the basement, from the fresh milk, eggs and churned butter in the kitchen, from the nearby woodshed fairly groaning with dried stovewood for the cold nights to come, from the hay piled high in the watertight barn, from the smokehouse hung full of sausage and ham, from the cud-chewing ruminations of old Bright and Lion.

On the Gates farm Christmas is a holiday as it remains in our oldest dreams, and even the young evergreens down the hill grow slowly toward the day when they will play their part in the season's amplitude.

Terry Todd

Thoughts From a Snowed-in Cabin

December 1983: In a few days it will be Christmas. I have been snowed in for several days here in my cabin in the Ozarks, but that is of no account. The lane is a county road, and after the school bus routes have been cleared, the man who drives the township grader may clear my way. But the machine is undependable and held together with baling wire and Ozark ingenuity, so it may not get here before the snow melts.

Fifteen years ago I was working in a city and had an hour's drive to work each day. I grew to loathe winter, dreading the drive on slippery, congested highways. But now I am a commercial honey producer and am off the road in winter. Instead, I repair equipment, label honey jars, prepare for the spring bee season and putter around in the barn or cabin. Winter is no longer an enemy. It has become a time of quiet and peace.

The mailman is going to try to make it today, so I'll walk down to the mailbox later. When the drifts are hip high, as they are today, I urge the dogs to break a path, but they look at me wisely and pretend that they are too loyal and obedient to do anything but walk at my heels. Pantywaist dogs, I scold. That makes them wag their tails happily. Are they my dogs or am I their human?

My son phoned from Boston and asked what I was going to do for Christmas. I declared the pine outside the three big windows in the living room to be my Christmas tree and hung suet on it as a gift to the blue jays, the nuthatches and the red-bellied woodpeckers. The feeder with birdseed on it goes across those windows, and the usual birds are feeding there — juncos, cardinals, titmice, tree sparrows and finches, both purple and gold.

Inside, the dogs and cats are luxuriating in the warmth of the wood stove. The public radio station outdoes itself during Christmas week. Last night I heard Bach's *B Minor Mass*. It feels snug and cheerful and peaceful here.

I see a white-breasted nuthatch in my Christmas tree. He has spotted the suet, and has seen the red-bellied woodpeckers feeding on it. It won't be long until his curiosity and need to eat overcome his caution. I'm glad I'll be here to see that. Witnessing it will be a Christmas gift in return.

Sue Hubbell

What Do Our Hearts Treasure?

Until a couple of years ago, the Christmases I have known have been in lands of the fir tree and pine. The same is true of my wife, who is a New Englander and whose Christmases have been observed in a cold setting, Bostonian in design. But times change, circumstances alter, health glides slowly downhill, and there is, of course, Christmas in lands of the palm tree and vine — which is what we were up against last month. Our Christmas, 1965, was spent in a rented house on the edge of a canal in Florida, locally called a bayou.

I knew there would have to be certain adjustments, emotional and physical, but I guess I was not quite prepared for them.

The house we walked into had been engaged sight unseen, and this is always fun and full of jolts, like a ride at an amusement park. Our pleasure palace was built of cinder blocks and was painted shocking pink. The principal tree on the place was a tall power pole sprouting transformers; it stood a few feet from the canal and threw a pleasant shade across the drive. The house itself, we soon discovered, was wonderfully supplied with labor-saving appliances and almost completely bare of any other sort of furnishing. There was no ice bucket, no water pitcher, no rugs on the terrazzo floors, no pictures on the pastel walls, no bookshelves, no books, and no garbage pail.

Several days before Christmas, I began to notice that my wife was suffering from crying spells, all of them of short duration. "It's Vietnam that is making me feel this way," she said. But I did not believe it was Vietnam. I knew her well enough, in her December phase, to know that something far deeper than Southeast Asia was at work.

I was too busy to cry. There was a man that came each day to work on the collapsed heating system. He was from a firm called "Air Comfort" and was a fine, brave, taciturn man. I would find him in a kneeling position, as though he were a figure in a creche, gazing at the tangle of tubes and wires left by the removal of a burned-out compressor. He kept his own counsel and did what he could, hour after hour, to remedy an almost impossible situation. I felt that if I hung around him long enough, I might catch the drift of the reverse-cycle system and pick up a crumb or two of knowledge that would stand me in good stead later on. The weather held good, and we were not really cold. The sunsets were spectacular. But the sun always sank behind the Australian pines and the palms on the opposite shore, and I knew that my wife and I were, unconsciously, watching it descend in its more familiar rim behind the birches, the black spruces, the firs, the hackmatacks across the road from our house in Maine.

Like everything else in Florida, the birds seemed inappropriate. I happen to admire the mourning dove, but by no stretch of the eardrum can its lament be called Christmassy. I like to see the turkey buzzard wheeling in the sky, but he is not a merry bird; his vigil is for the dying.

There arrived in the mail a program of the Christmas ceremony in the school at home, reporting that our youngest grandson had appeared in a pageant called "Goodbye to Last Year's Toys," and that our granddaughter had recited something called "What Do Our Hearts Treasure?"

There was very little traffic in the canal. Once in a while a pint whiskey bottle would float slowly by on the outgoing tide. Sometimes, toward the end of the day, a little green heron showed up and

fished from a mangrove that overhung the water. The scene was idyllic. Christmas was in the air, yet the air seemed too soft to sustain it.

In the vast shopping centers that ringed the city, Santa, in jumbo size, dominated the parking lots. In the commanding noonday sun, with the temperature in the seventies, he seemed vastly overdressed in his red suit with the ermine trimming — a saint who perspired under the arms. Through the arcades in front of the shops sauntered an endless procession of senior citizens, with their sad faces, their painful joints, their last-minute errands.

I went on an errand of my own. I visited a nursery and bought a poinsettia plant, hoping to introduce a spot of the correct color into our house. In the North, this errand would have enjoyed a certain stature, but in Florida the thing seemed faintly ridiculous. Driving away from the nursery with my prize, I passed a great forest of poinsettias blooming naturally in somebody's front yard. It seemed to take the point out of my purchase. A lot of things are red in Florida — the powder-puff bush, the red hibiscus, the red bougainvillaea, the cannas — all these blooms make a monkey out of a husband carrying home a small red potted plant.

We talked over the matter of the tree and decided that the traditional Christmas tree would be silly under these circumstances. We would get, we said, a tropical thing of some sort that would look good all winter. The nursery came up with a cluster of three little palmlike trees called *Dracaena marginata* (the man called it *imaginata*, which I liked better). When the plant was delivered, a small chameleon arrived with it and soon made the living room his own. He liked the curtain on the south wall, and would poke his evil little head out and join us for cocktails. I named him Beppo. Everyone admired our plant. The crying spells ceased, but it was plain there was still something the matter; it wasn't Vietnam, it wasn't the reverse-cycle system, it was some kind of unreality that pervaded our lives.

A large package arrived from the North on the twenty-second and I noted the familiar handwriting of our daughter-in-law. I carried the package into the living room, dumped it on the sofa, slit its throat with my jackknife, and left it for my wife to dissect. (She is methodical at Christmas and keeps a record of gifts and donors.) Soon I heard a sharp cry. "Come here! Look!" I found her standing on the hearth with her nose buried in a branch from a balsam fir, which she had hung over the fireplace. With it hung a harness strap of sleigh bells. The branch had un-

questionably been whacked from a tree in the woods behind our son's house in Maine and had made the long trip south. It wore the look and carried the smell of authenticity. "There!" said my wife, as though she had just delivered a baby.

The package also disgorged a tiny red drum and two tiny drumsticks, made from bright red wrapping paper by a grandchild. And the package contained school photographs, which we eagerly studied. Our youngest grandson had done something odd with his mouth, in a manly attempt to defeat the photographer, and looked just like Jimmy Hoffa. "How marvelous!" said my wife.

We placed the toy drum at the base of the *Dracaena marginata*. I constructed one small cornucopia out of the same bright red paper and hung it on a spiky frond of the tree. I fashioned a five-pointed star, strung it on a length of monofilament from my tackle box, and suspended it from the ceiling above the tree. The star revolved slowly, catching the light at intervals — a holy mobile. The tree now seemed biblical and just right. We were in business at last. I gazed out to where the soft and feathery Australian pines were outlined against the bright sky. They had hardened up momentarily for this hour of splendor. They were spruce! They were birch! They were fir! Everywhere, everywhere, Christmas tonight!

E.B. White

A Kind of Miracle

Trees just do not grow up here on the high plateaus of the Rockies — everybody knows that. Trees need good soil and good weather and up here there's no soil and terrible weather. People do not live here. Nothing can live up here and certainly not trees. That's why the tree is a kind of miracle.

The tree is a juniper, and it grows beside U.S. Highway 50 utterly alone, not another tree for miles. Nobody remembers who put the first Christmas ornament on it — some whimsical motorist of years ago. From that day to this, the tree has been redecorated each year. Nobody knows who does it. But each year, by Christmas day, the tree has become a Christmas tree.

The tree, which has no business growing here at all, has survived against all the odds. The summer droughts somehow haven't killed it, or the winter storms. When the highway builders came out to widen the road they could have taken the tree with one pass of their bulldozer. But some impulse led them to start widening the road just a few feet past the tree. The trucks pass so close that they rattle the tree's branches. The tree has also survived the trucks.

The tree violates the laws of man and nature. It is too close to the highway for man, and not far enough away for nature. The tree pays no attention. It is where it is. It survives.

People who live in Grand Junction, 30 miles one way, and in Delta, Colorado, 15 miles the other way, all know about and love the tree. They have Christmas trees of their own, of course, the kind of trees that are brought to town in trucks and sold in vacant lots and put up in living rooms. This one tree belongs to nobody and to everybody.

Just looking at it makes you think about how unexpected life on earth can be. The tree is so lonely and so brave that it seems to offer courage to those who pass it — and a message. It is the Christmas message: that there is life and hope even in a rough world.

Charles Kuralt

Come Christmas

You see this Christmas tree all silver gold?
It stood out many winters in the cold,

with tinsel sometimes made of crystal ice,
say once a winter morning — maybe twice.

More often it was trimmed by fallen snow
so heavy that the branches bent, with no

one anywhere to see how wondrous is
the hand of God in that white world of his.

And if you think it lonely through the night
when Christmas trees in houses take the light,

remember how his hand put up one star
in this same sky so long ago afar.

All stars are hung so every Christmas tree
has one above it. Let's go out and see.

David McCord

TEXT CREDITS

We thank these publishers, authors, or their representatives for permission to reprint their material.

The Ancients (p. 5), copyright © 1979 by Barbara Dodge Borland, as executor of the estate of Hal Borland. Reprinted by permission of Frances Collin, literary agent.

Wild Things (p. 7) from *Wild Things* by Dion Henderson, published by Tamarack Press, 1979.

The Enduring Evergreens (pp. 11-12), © 1985 by the National Wildlife Federation, adapted from *National Wildlife* magazine, January, 1985.

The Christmas Tree Tradition (pp. 17-20), excerpted from *The Christmas Tree Book*, by Phillip Snyder. Copyright © 1976 by Phillip Snyder. Reprinted by permission of Viking Penguin Inc.

For Allan (p. 22) from *Robert Frost: Poetry and Prose*, edited by Edward Connery Lathem and Lawrance Thompson. Copyright © 1972 by Holt, Rinehart and Winston, Inc. Reprinted by permission of the publisher.

"little tree" (p. 24), reprinted from TULIPS & CHIMNEYS by E. E. Cummings by permission of Liveright Publishing Corp. Copyright 1923, 1925, and renewed 1951, 1953 by E. E. Cummings. Copyright © 1973, 1976 by the trustees of the E. E. Cummings Trust and George James Firmage.

Francie's Christmas Tree (pp. 27-30), condensed from *A Tree Grows in Brooklyn* by Betty Smith. Copyright © 1943, 1947 by Betty Smith. Reprinted by permission of Harper & Row, Publishers, Inc.

Of Ox Bells and Christmas (pp. 33-35), condensed by permission of Terry Todd. Originally appeared in *Sports Illustrated*, Dec. 24, 1984.

Thoughts from a Snowed-in Cabin (p. 37), condensed by permission of Sue Hubbell. Originally appeared in *Sports Illustrated*, Dec. 24, 1984.

What Do Our Hearts Treasure? (pp. 39-41). Condensation of "What Do Our Hearts Treasure?" from *Essays of E. B. White* by E. B. White. Copyright © 1966 by *The New Yorker* and E. B.

White. Reprinted by permission of Harper & Row, Publishers, Inc.

A Kind of Miracle (p. 42), reprinted by permission of Charles Kuralt. Originally broadcast for "On the Road with Charles Kuralt," CBS.

Come Christmas (p. 45), from *One at a Time* by David McCord. Copyright © 1965, 1966 by David McCord. By permission of Little, Brown and Company.

PICTURE CREDITS

Cover: Quilt courtesy of Sharon Yenter/photo by Carl Murray. **1:** Freshly cut Christmas trees in a horse-drawn sleigh by Richard W. Brown. **2:** Victorian Christmas tree by Jon Riley/Folio, Inc. **4-5:** Snowy Washington forest by Steven C. Wilson/Entheos. **6:** Cougar in Wisconsin by Daniel J. Cox. **8-9:** Illustration by Frank Fretz. **10-11:** Frost-laden Engelman spruce forest by Daniel J. Cox. **13:** Short-eared owl in spruce by W. Perry Conway. **14-15:** Elk feeding in Wyoming by C.C.

Lockwood. **16:** Painting by Viggo Johansen (l851-l935)/Hirsch Sprungske Collection/Bridgeman Art Library. **18:** Glass butterfly ornament courtesy of Old World Christmas, P.O Box 8000, Spokane, WA. 99203. **19:** Embossed cardboard elephant ornament from *The Christmas Tree Book* by Phillip Snyder. Color illustrations copyright © 1976 by Phillip Snyder in all countries of the International Copyright Union. All rights reserved. Reprinted by permission of Viking Penguin Inc. **21:** National Christmas tree by Everett C. Johnson. **22-23:** Illustration by Bob Byrd. **25:** Illustration by Carolyn Croll. **26-27, 30-31:** Illustrations by Ted Lewin. **32, 35:** Oxen by Jose Azel/Contact Press Images. **36-37:** Cardinal by Robert P. Carr. **38:** Illustration by Jeffrey L. Dever/Dever Design. **43:** Colorado roadside Christmas tree by Al Gibes. **44-45:** Snowy forest by Art Wolfe. **48:** Cartoon by Edward Koren. **Endsheets** by Susan Sanford/MedSciArt Co.

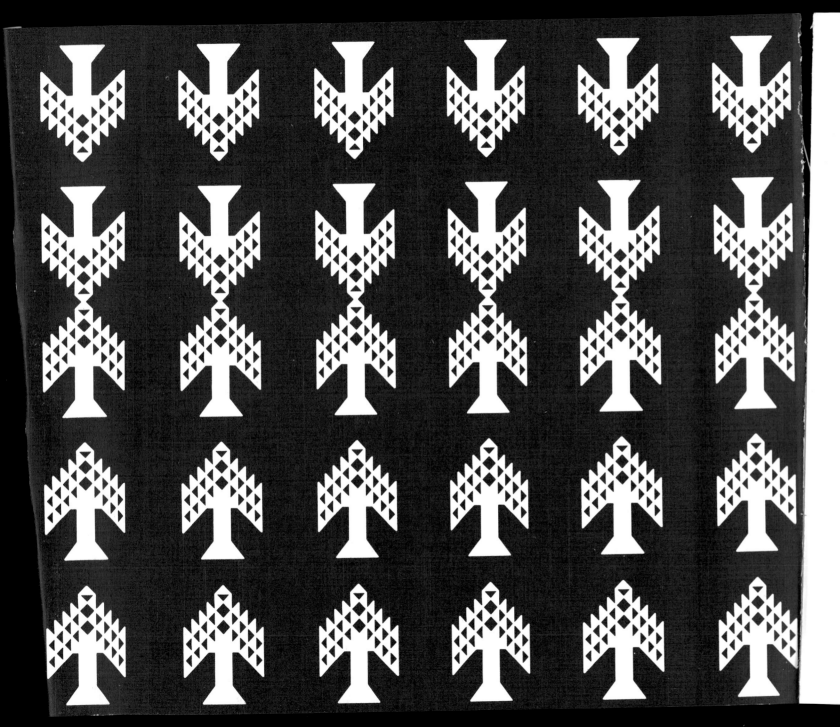

Library of Congress CIP Data

Main entry under title:
Trees of Christmas.

p. cm. — (Gifts of nature)

Contents:—The ancients /by Hal Borland—Wild things/by Dion Henderson —Natural history of ever-greens—History of Christ-mas trees/by Philip Snyder— "For Allan"/by Robert Frost —A tree grows in Brook-lyn/by Betty Smith—Of ox bells and Christmas/by Terry Todd—A tree for the birds/ by Sue Hubbell—What do our hearts treasure?/by E. B. White—"Little tree"/by e. e. cummings—The Christmas tree (Delta, Colorado)/by Charles Kuralt—"Come Christmas"/by David Mc-Cord.

ISBN 0-912186-92-5

1. Christmas trees—United States. 2. Christmas trees—United States—Literary collections.
I. Series.

GT4989.5.T74 1988
394.2'68282—dc 19 88-4864

About the Cover

The quilt design is called *Pine Tree*. To early settlers, the towering New England white pines guarded their cabins both physically and psychologically, helping the newcomers withstand winter winds and loneliness. The pine tree, then, presented a perfect subject for quilt-makers later on.

Many Pine Tree quilts date from the late 1800s, a time when thousands of pio-neers were heading west-ward. The pines may have reminded them of the New England homes they had left behind.

Staff for this Book

Howard F. Robinson *Editorial Director*

Elaine S. Furlow *Senior Editor*

Donna Miller *Design Director*

Holly Ritland *Designer*

Debby Anker *Illustrations Editor*

Michele Morris *Editorial Assistant*

Paul Wirth *Quality Control*

Margaret E. Wolf *Permissions Editor*

Tina Isom *Production Artist*

KOREN

48

Library of Congress CIP Data

Main entry under title:
Trees of Christmas.

p.   cm. — (Gifts of nature)
Contents:—The ancients /by Hal Borland—Wild things/by Dion Henderson —Natural history of evergreens—History of Christmas trees/by Philip Snyder— "For Allan"/by Robert Frost —A tree grows in Brooklyn/by Betty Smith—Of ox bells and Christmas/by Terry Todd—A tree for the birds/ by Sue Hubbell—What do our hearts treasure?/by E. B. White—"Little tree"/by e. e. cummings—The Christmas tree (Delta, Colorado)/by Charles Kuralt—"Come Christmas"/by David McCord.
ISBN 0-912186-92-5
1. Christmas trees— United States.   2. Christmas trees—United States— Literary collections.
I. Series.

GT4989.5.T74 1988
394.2'68282—dc 19   88-4864

About the Cover

The quilt design is called *Pine Tree*. To early settlers, the towering New England white pines guarded their cabins both physically and psychologically, helping the newcomers withstand winter winds and loneliness. The pine tree, then, presented a perfect subject for quiltmakers later on.

Many Pine Tree quilts date from the late 1800s, a time when thousands of pioneers were heading westward. The pines may have reminded them of the New England homes they had left behind.

Staff for this Book

Howard F. Robinson *Editorial Director*

Elaine S. Furlow *Senior Editor*

Donna Miller *Design Director*

Holly Ritland *Designer*

Debby Anker *Illustrations Editor*

Michele Morris *Editorial Assistant*

Paul Wirth *Quality Control*

Margaret E. Wolf *Permissions Editor*

Tina Isom *Production Artist*

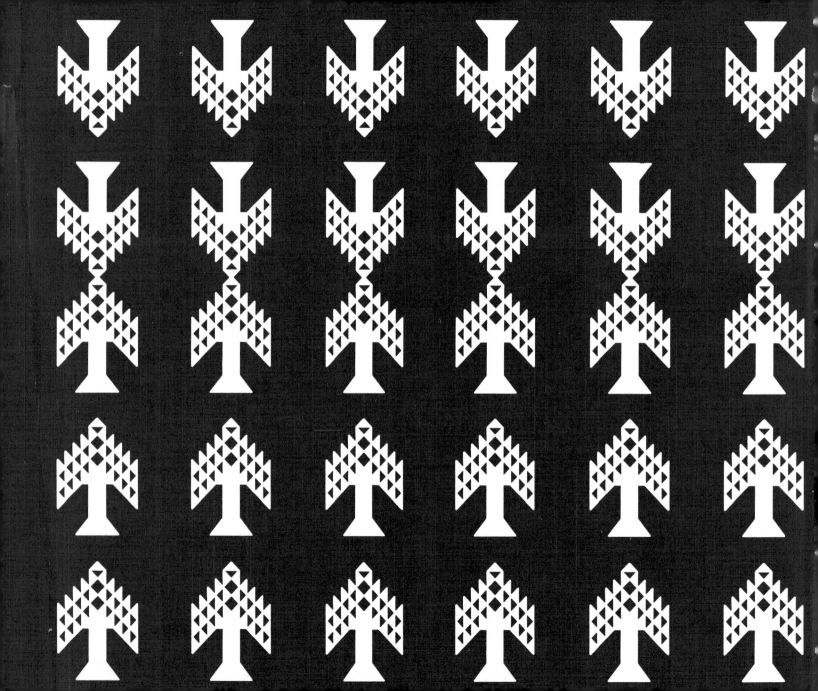